THE
SPLENDOR
OF THE
SAINTS

Mini-Study of the Lives of the Saints of the Orthodox Church

Written and Illustrated by:
Maria Athanasiou

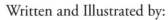

Then he said to Jesus, "Lord, remember me when You come into Your kingdom."
And Jesus said to him, "Assuredly, I say to you, today you will be with Me in Paradise." Luke 23:42-43 NKJV

WestBow Press books may be ordered through booksellers or by contacting:

WestBow Press
A Division of Thomas Nelson & Zondervan
1663 Liberty Drive
Bloomington, IN 47403
www.westbowpress.com
1 (866) 928-1240

Interior Graphics/Art Credit: Maria Athanasiou

ISBN: 978-1-9736-8291-2 (sc)
ISBN: 978-1-9736-8292-9 (e)

Library of Congress Control Number: 2019921160

Print information available on the last page.

WestBow Press rev. date: 01/22/2020

WestBow
PRESS®
A DIVISION OF THOMAS NELSON
& ZONDERVAN

To Glorify God and Honor the Saints.

The Saints are the friends of God. They loved the Lord exceedingly and made a complete commitment to Him. When we study their lives, we learn and benefit from them. We will love them and admire their achievements. We can also ask them for their intercessions and their help because the grace of God is in their holy relics.

May the Lord Jesus Christ continue to bless the hands of Maria Athanasiou, to tell beautifully, in words and images, the story of our Saviour and of His Saints and Angels, for the guiding of our Orthodox Christian children and their families!

Archimandrite Maximos

Maria's other Christian Picture books are:

Rejoice, The Nativity of our Lord Jesus Christ
The Amazing Life of Jesus Christ, The Three Years of His Ministry
The Virgin Mary Mother of God
Christ is Risen
The Holy Apostles
www.theholyapostlesbymaria.com

Acknowledgements:

I want to thank the following monks for their encouragement, and also for their input regarding written content and artwork: Archimandrite Maximos, Igumen Silouan, and Hierodeacon Parthenios of the Monastery of Saint Dionysios the Areopagite, Saint James, NY.

FOREWORD

What is the Purpose of my Life?

Children are often asked: "What would you like to be when you grow up?"

"A doctor!" "A scientist!" "A pilot!" "A musician!" "An artist!" The answers will vary, but each child will blurt out whatever has captured his or her imagination at the moment. Some will reach their goals; some will not. The difficulties and disappointments of life might lead a person to dismiss his goal as an impossible dream. Nevertheless, sooner or later, each of us is faced with an inescapable question. "What is the purpose of my life?" Whether we are children or adults, even if our goals have changed, that question persists.

The answer is simple but challenging: to become a saint. We often forget this lofty calling that is our real destiny. We need to be reminded over and over: the main goal of our life is our union with God, to become partakers of the divine nature." (2 Peter 1:4) We reach this goal only through our cooperation with God, through His power, and the intercessions of those who have triumphed in their struggle to attain the goal, the saints themselves.

This book of the life of the saints, written and illustrated by Maria Athanasiou, is a labor of love. It will help each of us keep the purpose of our life in mind. As a multitude of beautiful stars in the vast firmament of Heaven, each saint shines with their unique and awe-inspiring splendor. Soldiers, kings, queens, doctors, ascetics, bishops, married men and women, monks and nuns… Not one of them is the same, yet they all undividedly partake of the Uncreated Light. They remind us that no matter where we find ourselves in life, no matter what path we have taken as our vacation or profession, we can transfigure it into a *holy* way of life, imbued with meaning.

Even those who have grown up still have a chance to pursue and aspire towards a glorious goal. It is not just a naïve dream; rather, it is a reality confirmed by the "great cloud of witnesses" (Hebrews 12:1) abiding in Heaven and perpetually interceding for us. It is not too late to become children – humbly reliant on God – to attain the purpose of our life. For, "Except ye be converted, and become as little children, ye shall not enter into the kingdom of heaven" (Matthew 18:3).

Archimandrite Maximos

Abbot of Monastery of St. Dionysios the Areopagite
Saint James, NY

SAINT ALYPIUS THE ICONOGRAPHER

Alypius was a Russian iconographer and a Hieromonk at the Kiev Caves Monastery. He studied the iconography of the Greek Masters and beautified the church of the Dormition of the Theotokos. Alypius painted icons only to serve God. Many of his icons were miraculous, and sometimes angels helped him to paint them. Saint Alypius had the gift of miracle working and healing the sick.

Once a pious Christian commissioned Alypius to paint the icon of the Dormition of the Theotokos. He wanted the icon to be ready on August 15, the day of the feast. Alypius fell ill, and the man was worried because it was already the eve of the Holiday, and the icon was not finished. Alypius said to him, "Do not worry, my child, but trust in the Lord and know that the Lord can paint the icon of His Mother with one word."

Late that night, behold! A young man in white, and shining like the sun, appeared at the door. He went quietly near the unfinished icon and started to paint. He first applied the gold background. Then he applied the colors with amazing speed. In three hours he finished the whole icon. Then he turned to Alypius and asked him if he liked the icon. Alypius said, "You did the icon beautifully, my angel, with the grace of God." Then the angel took the icon in his hands and disappeared.

That morning of August 15, the holy icon was at the Church. When the man who was waiting for the icon arrived at the Church and saw it there, he remembered the words of Alypius to trust always in the Lord, and he fell on his knees and venerated the icon.

A couple of days later they visited Alypius and asked him who painted the icon. Alypius said, "An angel of God painted the icon during the night. He also took it to the Church. And behold look! The same angel is standing now here next to me waiting to take my soul. Can you see him?" It was August 17, 1114 AD. Saint Alypius' feast day is August 17.

SAINT ALYPIUS

2

GREAT MARTYR ANASTASIA OF ROME

The Deliverer from Potions

Anastasia was born in the 2nd century AD in Rome, during the reign of Emperor Diocletian, to a wealthy family. Her parents, Pretextatos and Fausta, were pious Christians. Saint Anastasia was well educated. Her teacher was saint Chrysogonus. He taught her the Word of God, and she was baptized Christian.

Since very young she was married to Popliona, a Roman Archon who was worshiping idols. Anastasia was very beautiful, wise, and kind. She also had a loving and humble heart and wanted to help the needy and hurting Christians. She was helping them secretly because she did not want her husband to know. Dressed with simple clothes she was going during the night to the hospitals and the prisons, where the martyrs of Christ were, bringing them food, clothes and money.

She visited them without fear. She took care of their wounds and gave them courage. Her husband was very angry when he learned that she was a Christian. Since then he did not let her out of the house. After he died, she continued to help the needy, until she was arrested. In prison, she continued to hymn and praise the Lord.

With her prayers, and with the grace of God, Saint Anastasia healed diseases, and delivered many from poison, this is why they called her "deliverer from potions" in Greek pharmakolitria. Anastasia is a synonym of Anastasis (Resurrection). She died in a bonfire on December 25. The Church remembers and celebrates her memory on December 22.

SAINT ANASTASIA OF ROME

MA

4

SAINT ANTONY THE GREAT

Father of Monks

Antony was born in Egypt in 251 AD, of pious and wealthy parents. Once when he was in the Church, he heard the Gospel and the words of Jesus saying, *"If you want to be perfect, go, sell what you have and give it to the poor, and you will have treasure in heaven; and come, follow Me."* Matthew 19:21 NKJV

Dedicated to follow the teaching of the Lord, when his parents died, he gave his wealth to the poor, and after he made sure his younger sister was safe in a convent, he left for the desert outside Alexandria. There he imitated St John the Baptist and lived alone with God as his only companion.

He planted a garden and baked bread every 6 months. He trained himself to fast and pray. When he thought of the eternal punishment, he prayed to the Lord to show him the road to salvation. Then an Angel appeared and showed him how to work and pray to attack evil thoughts and be saved.

He struggled against the passions and perfected himself in the virtues. He fought the demons and the devil with prayer and with the Psalms. In 335 he went to Alexandria and defended Orthodoxy against the heretical Arians and turned many unbelievers to Christ. Once he had a vision of Jesus who healed him from his wounds.

St Athanasius (Bishop of Alexandria 293-373) knew Antony personally and wrote a book about his life titled, "The Life of Antony". People followed Antony for advice, and his words were collected in "The Sayings of the Desert Fathers." In his old age Antony remained healthy, could see very well, had all his teeth, and was strong in his hands and his legs. He lived to be 105. His feast day is January 17.

"Seek humility, for it will cover all your sins," said Saint Antony.

SAINT ANTONY THE GREAT

I saw the snares of the Devil laid out upon the ground and I asked who can flee from these? An Angel said to me: Humility

6

SAINT ARSENIOS OF CAPPADOCIA

Theodoros (later named Arsenios) was born in Farasa, a small village of Cappadocia, in 1840 AD, from pious parents and had a brother named Vlasios. At a very young age they were left orphans and an aunt raised them.

Once Theodoros was drowning and Saint George appeared and miraculously saved him. That miracle was the reason Theodoros became a monk and Vlasios became a teacher of Byzantine Music to glorify God.

Arsenios had great love for God and for all God's creation. He especially loved the animals. In all human beings he saw the icon of God. Every Wednesday and every Friday he was fasting and praying on his knees. His face had a brilliant shine from prayer and fasting. He walked barefoot. He lived in the world but at the same time away from the world.

Saint Arsenios helped everyone even the Turks. He was able to heal the souls and bodies of people not with medicine but with the grace of God and with his prayers. He read prayers and psalms over the sick, and he never accepted money. In Farasa no one needed a doctor because all the villagers ran to him for healing. They called him Hatzi Effendi. Countless are the miracles he did, and he still is doing.

When he was 30, he became Archimandrite of Caesarea and strengthened all people in the Christian faith. He baptized Saint Paisios of Mount Athos and named him after himself, Arsenios. He was also his spiritual father. Saint Paisios had great respect for him and wrote a book about his life called, "Arsenios the Cappadocian."

God gifted Arsenios with foreknowledge. He knew the hour of his death. He died in 1924 in the Greek Island of Kerkira. He was 84. His feast day is November 10.

SAINT BASIL THE GREAT

Bishop of Caesarea From a Family of Saints

Basil was born in Caesarea of Cappadocia, Asia Minor in 330 AD to a wealthy family of pious Christians. His father was Saint Basil the Elder, his mother Saint Emily, his grandmother Saint Macrina the Elder, his older sister Saint Macrina a nun, his brothers Saint Gregory of Nyssa a Bishop, Saint Peter of Sebastia a Bishop, Naucratius a monk and Saint Theosebia his younger sister.

Basil received a good education. He studied medicine, astronomy, philosophy, grammar and rhetoric in Constantinople, and later in Athens, with his brother Gregory of Nyssa and his friend Gregory the Theologian.

Basil not only studied but also lived according to the Scriptures. He visited many monks in Egypt, Palestine, Syria and Mesopotamia to learn from them how to improve in the virtues and the ascetical life, and then he returned to Annesi in Caesarea and became a monk. In 370 he was elected Bishop of Caesarea and served the Church of Christ with unusual devotion for 8 years. He defended Holy Orthodoxy and fought against the heresy of Arius with the help of Saint Athanasius the Great.

He chose to live in poverty. He had humility and strong faith. He created hospitals, orphanages and old age homes. He had great wisdom and was a great teacher of the Word of God. He wrote liturgical prayers, Church songs, and many worthy writings about heavenly things. He wrote a Treatise on the Holy Spirit, speeches about the Six Days of Creation (Hexaemeron) and about the Psalms, and the Holy Liturgy of the Church which is celebrated ten times a year.

He is one of the three leaders or Hierarchs of the Church, together with Saint Gregory the Theologian and Saint John Chrysostom. His name Basil is a synonym with the royal flower that grew at the Cross of Jesus. He fell asleep in the Lord on January 1, 379 AD. He was 49. Basil is a spiritual giant who left behind a great spiritual work. His feast days are January 1 and January 30 (the celebration of the Three Hierarchs).

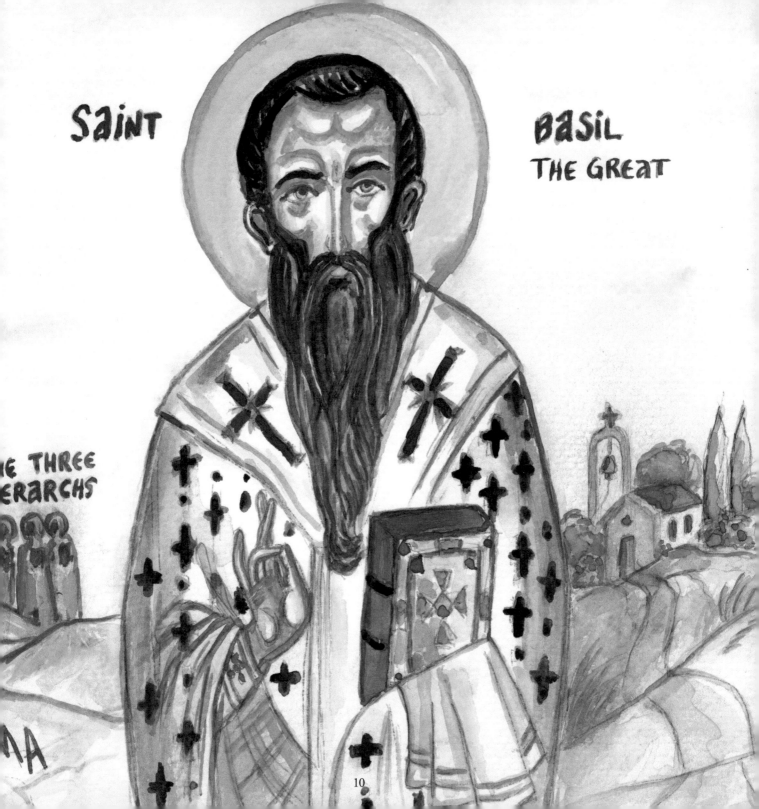

SAINT BASIL THE GREAT

THE THREE HIERARCHS

10

SAINT CATHERINE OF ALEXANDRIA

Catherine was born in Alexandria, the capital of Egypt and the center of Hellenistic knowledge, in about 300 AD, to a wealthy family. Her father, Constas, was the Governor of Alexandria, during the reign of Maximian. Catherine received excellent education and was intelligent, and very beautiful, but she refused to get married.

Once when Saint Catherine visited a spiritual father, he told her about the true God Jesus Christ and gave her an icon of the Virgin Mary holding Jesus. Catherine said she wanted to see Jesus, and she prayed all night to the Virgin Mary.

The Virgin Mary appeared to her in a dream, holding Jesus, but Jesus turned His face away from her and did not look at her. After Catherine was baptized, she had that dream again, and this time Jesus looked kindly at her and gave her a ring. When Catherine woke up, the ring was on her finger, and it still is on her finger today.

Saint Catherine loved God and had a strong faith. She was a Christian teacher and public speaker. She was very brave and converted many to Christianity. Catherine suffered many tortures and finally was beheaded because she defended Christ and refused to worship the idols.

According to tradition, her fragrant relics were taken by angels to Mount Sinai, the Holy Mountain where Moses saw the burning bush and heard the voice of God. Many miracles happen there. Visitors to the Monastery of St. Catherine receive a ring as a blessing. Her feast day is November 25.

Saint

CATHE
RINE

12

SAINT CHRISTINA OF TYRE

Christina was born in Tyre of Syria in the 3rd Century. Her father, Urban, was a wealthy pagan and the Governor of Tyre. Christina was very beautiful. Since she was very young, her father locked her in a tower full of golden idols and forced her to worship them.

Christina liked to look out of the windows of the tower. She was amazed at the blue sky and the shining sea and green grass and the trees and the colorful flowers and the birds of the air. She could see everything even though she was not allowed to go outside.

She was admiring that beauty all around when she was looking out of her window, and she was wondering in her heart who was the real Creator of all this beauty and of the whole world.

She did not like the speechless idols, and she started to pray secretly to the unknown God. She was asking God to reveal Himself to her. One day a miracle happened, when an angel sent by God appeared to her and told her all about the true God Jesus Christ.

Christina believed, and immediately she broke all the golden idols and gave all the gold pieces to the poor. Her father did not like that and became very angry. He gave orders to his servants to throw Christina in prison without food. Her mother visited her in jail and asked her to renounce Jesus, but Christina had great faith and she refused.

The angel visited her in prison and strengthened her. She endured many tortures because the angel was with her and healed her every time. They also threw her in the sea but angels helped her to walk on water. Jesus himself came, and after He baptized her, the angels brought her to the shore safely. Christina is a great martyr. Many witnesses of her martyrdom became Christians. The Church celebrates her memory on July 24.

SAINT CHRI STINA

14

SAINT DEMETRIUS AND SAINT NESTOR

Demetrius the Myrrh-gusher of Thessalonica

Demetrius was born of pious Christian parents in Illyricum, Thessalonica, in about 270 AD. He was a Chiliarch in the Roman army at age 22. The Roman Emperor Maximian, who had a harsh upbringing, appointed Demetrius to torture and kill the Christians. Instead Demetrius was a teacher of Christianity and had formed a Bible study group. For this he was kept prisoner in the bath house. An angel of the Lord appeared to Demetrius in jail and strengthened him.

Nestor, one of his students, was willing to fight Lyaeus, the giant wrestler, who was killing Christians. Nestor knew of the miracles Demetrius had the power to perform in the name of Jesus Christ, his God, and he visited Demetrius before the battle, asking for his help and his blessing. Demetrius prayed to Jesus and gave strength and courage to Nestor.

After Nestor had received the blessings from Saint Demetrius, he walked into the stadium, and before entering the arena to fight Lyaeus he sealed himself with the sign of the Cross and said, "O God of Demetrius, help me!" Nestor won the battle.

The Emperor Maximian was very angry, and he immediately gave orders to his soldiers to kill both Demetrius and Nestor. Demetrius is a Great Martyr, a Military Saint. He is often depicted in his icons on a red horse.

His relics began producing fragrant myrrh and many miracles and healings. He is the patron Saint of Thessalonica, and a great protector for all. The feast day of Saint Demetrius is October 26, and the feast day of Saint Nestor October 27.

SAINT GERASIMOS
The New Ascetic of Kefalonia

Gerasimos was born in Peloponnese, Greece, in 1506 AD, to a wealthy and devout family. His parents, Kale and Demetrius Notaras, were pious Christians and taught Gerasimos many virtues.

Since his youth, he studied the Holy Scriptures well and visited many monasteries in Greece, trying to learn from the other ascetics and spiritual fathers the virtues. He became a Monk on Mount Athos and later traveled to many places in Greece. He went also to Jerusalem, and there he was ordained a deacon, and then a priest by the Patriarch of Jerusalem.

He loved silence and searched for quiet places. He came to Zakynthos, where he lived in a mountain cave, in solitude and prayer. When people started to visit him for advice, to avoid praises, he went to Kefalonia, another island in the Ionian Sea. There he found an old church and worked hard to rebuild it. He called it New Jerusalem. He also made a monastery for women, which was a center for charities. Saint Gerasimos lived for many years struggling to perfect the virtues, with prayers, fasting, prostrations and vigils, and everyone loved him and went to church to hear his teaching.

God gave him the gift of working miracles. He healed many with incurable diseases and cast out unclean spirits. When there was no rain for a long time, he prayed on his knees, and the Lord answered his prayers and sent rain.

Saint Gerasimos knew the hour of his death. He died peacefully on August 15, 1570. His relics remain incorrupt, working many miracles of healing and giving off a fragrant myrrh. The church celebrates his memory twice a year, on August 16 and on October 20. On these Holidays there is a great celebration and a panigiri (festival) on the island.

SAINT GERACIMO OF KEFALONIA

CHILDREN SEEK PEACE AND HUMILITY

IC XC NI KA

MA

18

SAINT GREGORY PALAMAS

Archbishop of Thessalonica

Gregory was born in Constantinople in 1296 AD to Kalloni and Constantine. He was raised in the Emperor's palace, but early in his life he preferred poverty and went to Mount Athos to become a monk. He always studied the Holy Scriptures, and on Sundays he was a cantor in the church.

He struggled hard to achieve spiritual perfection and learned the discipline of "Hesychasm" or uninterrupted prayer, the prayer of the heart, which requires peace and solitude. This practice is also beneficial for one's health. Saint Paul taught to pray always without ceasing, and Saint Gregory explains how this is possible if we always pray mentally, in the spirit, in our mind, while we sit, or walk, or work with our hands, or eat, etc. This is true prayer, and it is pleasing to God, when the inner man is always in communication with Him.

Wise Gregory taught about the noetic watchfulness and purity of heart and enlightened all with his teaching. He was a luminary to the world, a herald of divine grace, a speaker, a philosopher, and a theological writer. His writings are treasuries of divine knowledge in the Philokalia. He also suffered to defend Orthodoxy, and he spent 4 years in prison. When he was released, he was elected Archbishop of Thessalonica.

He died in 1359. His last words before he died were, "To the heights! To the heights!" His holy relics are in the Cathedral of Thessalonica. The Church remembers him twice a year, on November 14, and also every 2nd Sunday of Great Lent, as a celebration of the victory of the Church over heresy because he defended Orthodoxy. His family is a family of saints. His four siblings are also canonized saints.

SAINT GREGORY PALAMAS

20

SAINT JOHN KUKUZELIS OR KOUKOUZELIS THE HYMNOGRAPHER

The Chanter of Great Lavra Monastery

John lived in the 14th Century AD. He was very talented, with an angelic voice. He studied music in Constantinople and was chosen to be the top singer in the imperial court. Later he went to Mount Athos to devote his life to God. He became a monk tending sheep. Out of humility, to avoid praises, he did not reveal that he was a singer.

When John was alone with the sheep in the wilderness, he was praying, singing hymns to the Lord and to the Theotokos. One day some monks heard him sing, and they thought they heard an angel from above singing with a voice so sweet.

When the abbot heard about it, he called John and told him never to hide the talent God gave him but to use it for the glory of God. Since then, John became the head Chanter of the Great Lavra monastery. He chanted from his soul, with humility and fear of God.

Once, after singing the Hymn "All creation rejoices" to the Theotokos, she appeared to him in his dream and told him: "Rejoice, John! Sing and don't stop singing; and for this I will never leave you." She then placed a gold coin into his hand and disappeared. When John woke up, the gold coin was in his hand. This coin is by the icon of the Theotokos called Kukuzelissa (after Kukuzelis) in the Monastery of Lavra. Many miracles occur with that golden coin.

They named him Kukuzelis because he was always fasting, and he was only eating beans and peas. Saint John Kukuzelis was a gifted singer and composer of Orthodox Church music. He lived a saintly life. He was always singing reverently beautiful hymns to God, and he never sat down in the church. The Virgin Mary appeared to John once again and healed him, when he was sick with pains in his legs from always standing. He is the patron Saint of Church Musicians. His feast day is October 1.

Saint
John
Kukuzelis

I WILL NEVER LEAVE YOU

22

SAINT NECTARIOS OF AEGINA

Metropolitan of Pentapolis

Anastasios was born in 1846 AD in Silyvria of Thrace. His parents Demos and Vasiliki Kephalas were not wealthy but were pious Christians, and they raised him to love God. Anastasios had a special attachment to his grandmother, who taught him many prayers. When he was 14, he traveled alone to Constantinople to find a job and go to school. He completed his studies in the University of Athens.

In the beginning, he worked as a teacher in the Island of Chios. Later he become a monk and was named Lazarus. When he became a deacon, he was named Nectarios. The Patriarch of Alexandria in Egypt, Sophronios, ordained him a priest, and Nectarios was elected Metropolitan of Pentapolis. He served with love and devotion and beautified the Church of Saint Nicholas.

People liked Nectarios for his sermons, his humility and his loving heart. The other priests were very jealous of him and accused him with many lies. As a result, Nectarios was suddenly dismissed. He returned to Athens with no money and no Church to serve. He suffered for a long time, without complaining. He did not fight back against his accusers; instead he prayed constantly.

After many sufferings, he was accepted to be the Director of the Rizarios School for Priests in Athens, where he stayed for 15 years. He retired to the Island of Aegina, where he built the Monastery of the Holy Trinity for women, and spent the last years of his life.

Saint Nectarios wrote many theological sermons, books and Bible commentaries. He had visions of the Holy Theotokos and wrote many hymns to her including the hymn "Agni Parthene Despina." He became protector of Aegina, and he was a wonder worker. He worked many miracles. The hospital room where Saint Nectarios died is kept to this day as a place of veneration. His feast day is November 9.

SAINT NECTARIO

SAINT NEPHON
Bishop of Constantia

Nephon was born in Paphlagonia of Asia Minor, during the time of Constantine the Great (280-337 AD). His father, Agapetos, sent him to Constantinople to study, from a very young age. There he received a good education. He was a kind child, and he had a special love for the poor. He liked to attend Church, but in the years of his youth, he was trapped in the company of immoral friends in the big city, and he lived a very sinful life.

One day Nephon realized his life style was not proper, and he repented. He started to fight against his passions, and struggled with prayer and fasting, asking God continuously to give him a humble heart and to save him. With God's grace, he overcame the attacks of the devil.

Nephon became a monk. Later, Patriarch Alexander of Alexandria made him the bishop of Constantia, on the island of Cyprus. Nephon built a Church to the Most Holy Theotokos in Constantinople.

The Lord granted him to see many divine visions. One night while he was alone praying, he had a prophetic vision of the future Judgment Day. He saw the Lord Jesus Christ in the sky surrounded by many angels. He saw angels and spoke with them. Nephon was also able to see the departure of the soul after death, and he knew the time of his own death, three days before.

On the day of his departure, while he was burning with fever, he saw the Holy Apostles, many Saints, and the Most Holy Theotokos arrive by his side. Then the Lord Jesus Christ arrived, in a very bright shining light, to receive the soul of Nephon. Saint Athanasius the Great also arrived. He was informed supernaturally through divine revelation. The day Saint Nephon died was December 23. This is the day the Church celebrates his memory.

SAINT
NEPHON

MA

26

SAINT NICHOLAS THE WONDERWORKER
Archbishop of Myra in Lycia

Nicholas was born in Lycia of Asia Minor around 270 AD to a Christian and wealthy family. His parents Nonna and Theophanes sent him to receive a good education in the best Greek schools. Nicholas was an excellent student, and since very young age, he followed the canons of the Church and loved virtue. When his parents died, he gave all his inheritance to the poor and traveled by ship to Jerusalem, to devote his time to God and a life of prayer. On the way there, a big storm arose at sea. Saint Nicholas calmed the storm with his prayers and saved the ship.

In Myra he became a deacon, and later he was ordained the Archbishop. He helped the needy and gave alms in secret. Once he threw bags of gold into the window of a poor man's house to provide dowries for his daughters. He was blessed with the gifts of healing and wonder working.

He was one of the 318 Bishops at the Ecumenical Counsel of Nicaea of Bithynia in 325 AD. There he struck the heretic Arius in the face, because he spoke against Jesus and the All Holy Theotokos. According to the canon any bishop who would strike anyone should be deposed. That night the Lord Jesus and the Theotokos appeared to several bishops telling them not to depose him, because he had acted out of love for the truth.

The Virgin Mary appeared to him and gave him an omophorion, and the Lord Jesus appeared and gave him a Gospel covered with precious stones and commanded him to go back to serve the Church and save many souls.

Many times Saint Nicholas calmed storms with his prayers and saved ships. He liked solitude and silence. He died peacefully around 345 AD. His relics are flowing with healing myrrh. He is the patron saint for children, sailors and travelers. His feast day is December 6.

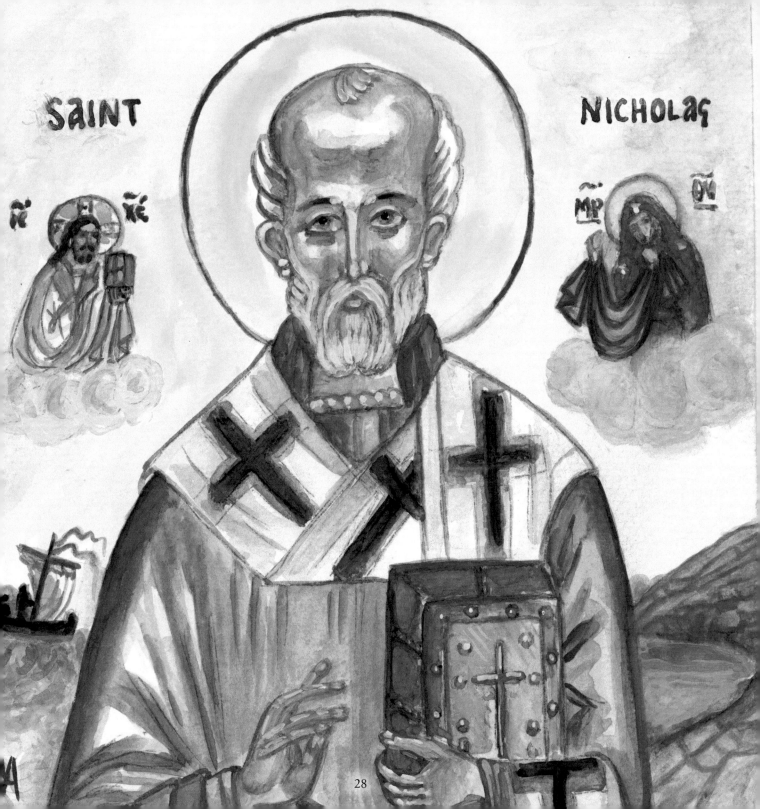

SAINT NICHOLAS

28

ONUPHRIUS OF EGYPT

The Desert Dweller

Onuphrius was born in Persia in the 4th century to a pious, royal couple. He grew up learning to obey the commandments of God, and he always studied the Bible. First he became a monk and later a hermit. He left for the desert to imitate the desert dwellers like the Prophet Elijah and Saint John the Forerunner.

When he was walking in the desert, he saw his angel in a bright light next to him. The angel brought him to a cave that was near a tall palm tree and a fountain with crystal clear water. Onuphrius stayed in that cave for 60 years. He was praying constantly to God for all the world, and the Holy Spirit was with him and enlightened him. Onuphrius struggled to make his heart pure with spiritual discipline.

The animals were his friends, and his food was dates from the palm tree. On Saturday and Sunday an Angel came down and gave him Holy Eucharist and comforted him. Other times, the Angel took him to visit the heavenly places and to see the Saints.

Towards the end of his life, Saint Onuphrius was discovered by Saint Paphnutius.

Onuphrius knew the day his soul was leaving for the heavenly city. He prayed with tears before he gave his spirit into the hands of God. In his prayer he also asked God to protect from all evil any one who will celebrate his memory or write about his life.

Saint Paphnutius, who was present to bury him, heard angels singing hymns, and there was great gladness when Onuphrius went to meet God. After Saint Paphnutius buried him, he wanted to stay in that cave, but the palm tree fell down, and the fountain dried up as a sign that he should go back to the world and tell all about Onuphrius. Saint Onuphrius' feast day is June 12.

SAINT

ONU
PHRI
U

iNT
PHNUTIUS

HAVE
MEMORY
OF
YOUR
OWN
EXIT

MA

30

HOLY GREAT MARTYR AND
HEALER PANTELEIMON

Pantaleon, that means in Greek, "in all things a lion", was born in Nicomedia of Asia Minor in about 275 AD, from an idolater father and a Christian mother. His mother died when he was a young boy, and his father sent him to pagan schools where he studied medicine with the famous doctor Efrosinos.

Pantaleon became Christian when he was already a successful doctor, after he met the priest Hermolaos, who was also a saint, and who taught him about Jesus. He believed and was baptized. After his father died, Pantaleon freed his slaves and gave all his wealth to the poor.

He healed the sick that came to him, with prayer and through the grace of God, rather than through medicine, and he did not accept any money. He also taught his patients the Christian faith and converted many to Christianity. He is a Holy Unmercenary, meaning not accepting any payment. He was intelligent, kind and meek.

Other physicians were very jealous of him because everyone liked him. After he had healed a blind man, and later a paralytic miraculously through prayer in the name of the Lord Jesus Christ, they accused him to the Emperor Maximian of being a Christian. Maximian, who at that time was persecuting the Church of Christ, sentenced him to be tortured, because he refused to abandon his Christian faith.

He was called Panteleimon, which means in Greek, "one who has mercy and compassion for everyone". Saint Panteleimon suffered many tortures, but Jesus appeared to him and strengthened him during his suffering. He was beheaded in 304 AD. He intercedes to God on behalf of the sick, that the Great Physician himself, our Lord Jesus Christ, may heal and strengthen them. We celebrate his feast day on July 27.

SAINT PANTE LEIMON

32

SAINT PARASKEVI OF ROME

Martyr and Wonder Worker of Christ

Paraskevi was born in Rome in 130 AD. Her pious parents, Agathon and Politia had no children, and they always prayed to God asking for a child. Their prayers were answered with a little girl. She was born on a Friday, and they named her Paraskevi which is the Greek word for Friday, and it means preparation. They raised her to be a devout Christian as they promised God in their prayers.

Paraskevi liked to read the Holy Scriptures and to pray to God, imitating her parents. When they died, she gave her wealth to the poor, became a nun and devoted herself to teach the Word of God, imitating the Holy Apostles.

Paraskevi traveled in many places teaching the Gospel, and she brought many to Christ. When she was in the small village of Asia Minor, Therapia, the idolater Emperor Antonius called her and asked her to renounce Christ and accept the idols, but when she refused, he gave orders to torture her and place her in a cauldron with hot oil.

Miraculously she was not burnt, and Antonius could not understand how she was not burnt. He asked her to throw some of that oil on him, because he did not think the oil was hot enough. Paraskevi threw some of that oil on his face, and he was blinded. He then cried for help, and Saint Paraskevi prayed to God and washed his eyes with water from the spring of Therapia, and his eye sight was immediately restored.

After this miracle, he freed her, and he was baptized. Paraskevi did many miracles with the sign of the Cross. The Holy Water of the Spring in Therapia is miraculous to this day. Therapia in Greek means healing. Saint Paraskevi is a doctor for the physical and the spiritual eyes. Her feast day is July 26.

SAINT PARASKEVI OF ROME

34

SAINTS RAPHAEL, NICHOLAS AND IRENE OF LESBOS

The New Martyrs of Christ

Saints Raphael, Nicholas, and Irene were unknown for 500 years after their martyrdom. In 1959, the Saints appeared to the people of Lesbos in dreams and visions and revealed to them their stories and guided them to find their graves. They said that they wanted to be remembered.

Many times, the villagers would see a monk walking on the hill, with a censer in his hand, and then a lightening would cover him, and he would disappear. According to tradition a monk was killed there by the Turks. Because of these appearances they named that hill Kalogeros, which is the Greek word for Monk.

Their relics were found and were fragrant. Many miracles happened in the Monastery and in other places. Photios Kontoglou, a master iconographer in Greece, wrote their icons according to the specific descriptions, and a Liturgy was composed for them, in Mount Athos.

George Lascarides was born in Ithaca, Greece, to a Christian family. He served in the army as Chiliarch and went to the University of France to study theology. There he met fellow student Nicholas, from Thessalonica. They became friends and together they returned to Athens. George became a monk and a priest and received the name Raphael, and Nicholas became a deacon.

Later they went together to the Island of Mytilini, to Thermi, to the Monastery of the Panagia of Karyes, to escape from the Turks. They lived there many years, serving God and praying always, until the Turks arrived and tortured and killed them. Irene was a 12 year old girl, one of the many martyrs for Christ that day. It was April 9, 1463.

The new martyrs of Christ, Saints Raphael, Nicholas, and Irene are a real proof of the Resurrection. The Church celebrates their memory on April 9.

SAINT
RAPHAEL

SAINT
NICHOLAS

SAINT
IRENE

IC XC
NI KA

THE
SOULS
OF THE
RIGHT
EOUS
ARE IN
GOD'S
HAND

MA

36

SAINT ROMANOS THE MELODIST

Romanos was born in the 5th century AD to a Jewish family in Emesa, Syria during the golden age of Byzantine hymnography and during the reign of King Anastasius.

He was baptized an Orthodox Christian and moved to Beirut, where he was ordained a deacon in the church of the Resurrection. According to legend he was not a talented singer or reader at first, but he had a strong faith and great love for the Theotokos. He was praying to her with contrition. Once, after such prayers to her on Christmas Eve, the Theotokos appeared to him in a dream holding a scroll. She offered it to him and told him to eat it. Then she disappeared.

Immediately after this dream, a great miracle happened. That night Romanos composed the hymn of the Nativity of Jesus Christ and was able to chant it beautifully in the Church the next day with a clear, sweet, angelic voice.

Saint Romanos was blessed with the gift of writing poems and music. He was a great Ecclesiastical poet, and he composed many hymns and kontakia for the Church by divine inspiration. He wrote the Akathist Hymn to the Theotokos, which is chanted as a devotion to the All-Holy Mother of God by the Orthodox Christians.

The Akathist Hymn is a beautiful service with praises to the Theotokos. Akathist means in Greek not sitting, and during the service of the Akathist Hymn all participants stand.

In icons, Saint Romanos is depicted wearing a short, red, choir-singer's robe, and he is placed in the center of the Church. He reposed in 556. The Church celebrates his memory on October 1.

MP ΘΥ

SAINT
ROMANS
THE
MELO
DIST

HOLY ✝ HOLY ✝ HOLY ✝ HOLY ✝

MA

38

SAINT SPYRIDON THE WONDERWORKER

Bishop of Trimythus in Cyprus

Spyridon was born in Cyprus in 270 AD to a family of shepherds. They were pious Christians, and they raised him to be faithful. Spyridon was a simple shepherd with a humble heart. His daily companion was the Holy Bible. He packed it with his lunch and read under the trees when he was watching his sheep. He always studied the Word of God. He married a Christian woman, and they had a daughter, whom they named Irene. After his wife died, he was elected Bishop of Trimythus, a village in Cyprus. When he was celebrating the Divine Liturgy, angels from heaven were present singing with him.

Spyridon was one of the 318 Fathers of the Church that participated in the First Ecumenical Council in 325 AD in Nicaea of Bithynia, which Constantine the Great called. Saint Spyridon fought the heresies of Arius against the Lord and the Virgin Mary. He also explained about the Holy Trinity. He said that this Mystery is not easily understood by our limited perception. Then he held a brick in his right hand and likened the three elements of the brick, fire, water and clay to the three Persons of the Holy Trinity, the Father, the Son and the Holy Spirit, one God undivided.

He was kind and gave alms and excelled in piety. For his piety he received blessings from above. God blessed him with the gift of healing. He performed many miracles with his intercessions and his prayers to the Lord.

Once he went to the grave of his daughter, asked her a question, and she gave him the answer. He never visited Corfu when he was alive, but his body was brought there for safety and is still there intact in a glass casket in a Church named after him. He departed peacefully from this life when he was about 80 years old. He is the defender of Corfu and a miracle worker. His feast day is December 12.

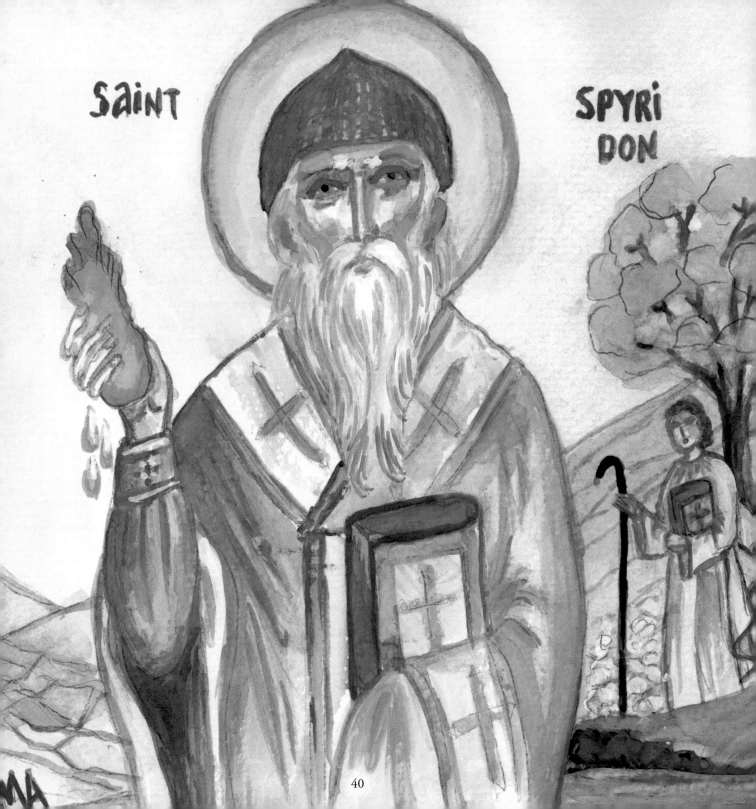

SAINT SPYRI DON

Printed in the United States
By Bookmasters